# BEAUTY SCHOOL ADMISSIONS : THE STATE OF FLORIDA

## MR. R. DOMINGUEZ, MIO-PSYCH

Beauty School Admissions - State of Florida

Copyright © 2023 Raul Dominguez
All rights reserved.
ISBN:9798854770040



Raul Dominguez
Miami FL, USA

# TABLE OF CONTENT

# PROLOGUE

Welcome to this journey; your go-to resource for mastering the art of admissions in the vibrant state of Florida's beauty industry. As aspiring beauty professionals, you are about to embark on a transformative journey that will not only hone your creative skills but also shape your career and passion for making others feel beautiful.

The state of Florida is a dynamic and thriving hub for the beauty industry, offering a multitude of opportunities across cosmetology, esthetics, nail technology, barbering, and more. Whether you dream of becoming a skilled hairstylist, a talented makeup artist, or an expert nail technician, this book is your ultimate training manual, guiding you from A to Z in the admissions process.

As an admission representative, your role is vital in helping prospective students navigate their way into the world of beauty education. Your expertise and knowledge hold the key to transforming lives and unlocking the doors to a fulfilling career in the beauty realm. This book is tailored to equip you with the tools and insights you need to excel in your role and support aspiring beauty professionals in realizing their dreams.

Within these pages, we will delve into the intricacies of beauty school admissions, from understanding the various types of beauty schools and their accreditations to comprehending the essential skills and traits that will set aspiring beauty professionals on a path to success. We will explore financial aid options, budgeting for beauty school education, and how to prepare for State Board Examinations with confidence.

Furthermore, we will unravel the diverse specializations and programs offered by beauty schools, helping you assist potential students in identifying their career goals and making informed decisions about their education. Along the way, we will share real-life examples, case studies, and valuable documentation required to ensure a seamless and rewarding admissions process.

As you journey through this book, envision yourself as a guiding light for aspiring beauty professionals in Florida. Your dedication to their success will make a lasting impact on their lives and the industry as a whole. Together, let's embark on this transformative adventure to create a thriving and inclusive beauty community in the Sunshine State.

So, are you ready to embark on the "Beauty Schools Admissions - State of Florida" and become a master of admissions in the state of Florida? Let's open the doors to a world of creativity, innovation, and endless possibilities. Your journey starts now!

# THE WORLD OF BEAUTY SCHOOLS

Congratulations on embarking on a journey into the captivating world of beauty schools! In this chapter, we introduce you to the exciting and diverse opportunities that await you in the beauty industry. From hairstyling and makeup artistry to nail technology and skincare, Florida's beauty schools offer a wide range of programs designed to unleash your creativity and passion for aesthetics.

## WHY CHOOSE FLORIDA FOR YOUR BEAUTY EDUCATION?

Discover why Florida is a sought-after destination for aspiring beauty professionals. Learn about the state's vibrant culture, booming beauty market, and how it fosters a nurturing environment for students pursuing careers in this dynamic field.

# UNDERSTANDING BEAUTY SCHOOLS IN FLORIDA

## TYPES OF BEAUTY SCHOOLS

Delve into the various types of beauty schools in Florida, such as cosmetology schools, esthetics schools, barbering schools, and more. Understand the differences between these institutions to make an informed choice that aligns with your career aspirations.

# TYPES OF BEAUTY SCHOOLS:

**Cosmetology Schools:**

Cosmetology schools offer comprehensive programs that cover a wide range of beauty services, including hair care, skincare, nail care, and makeup artistry. Students receive hands-on training in hair cutting, styling, coloring, chemical treatments, facials, waxing, and more. Cosmetology schools provide a well-rounded education for those aspiring to become versatile beauty professionals.

**Esthetics Schools:**

Esthetics schools focus specifically on skincare and facial treatments. Students learn about various skincare techniques, including facials, exfoliation, extractions, and chemical peels. They are trained to analyze skin types, address specific skin concerns, and provide customized skincare solutions to clients.

**Barbering Schools:**

Barbering schools concentrate on men's grooming and haircare. Students in barbering programs gain expertise in traditional and modern barbering techniques, such as haircuts, shaving, beard and mustache grooming, and hairstyling for men. The curriculum also covers scalp and facial treatments.

**Nail Technology Schools:**

Nail technology schools specialize in training students to become nail technicians. Nail techs learn the art of manicures, pedicures, nail art, and various nail enhancement techniques like acrylics, gels, and nail extensions. Emphasis is placed on nail health, sanitation, and maintaining the overall wellbeing of clients' nails.

**Makeup Artistry Schools:**

Makeup artistry schools focus on the art and application of makeup. Students learn various makeup styles, from natural and bridal makeup to high-fashion and special effects makeup. Makeup artistry programs often include instruction in color theory, contouring, highlighting, and using makeup to enhance facial features.

**Permanent Makeup Schools:**

Permanent makeup schools offer specialized training in micro-pigmentation techniques. Students learn to apply permanent makeup for eyebrows, eyeliner, lip color, and other facial enhancements. The curriculum covers the safe use of pigment and the importance of proper sterilization practices.

**Cosmetology Instructor Schools:**

Cosmetology instructor schools cater to individuals interested in teaching beauty-related subjects. Students learn effective teaching methods, curriculum development, and how to assess students' progress. Completion of a cosmetology instructor program is often required to become a licensed cosmetology instructor.

**Esthetics Instructor Schools:**

Similar to cosmetology instructor schools, esthetics instructor schools train individuals to become licensed esthetics instructors. The curriculum focuses on teaching advanced skincare techniques, esthetics theory, and classroom management.

Each type of beauty school serves a specific niche within the beauty industry, allowing students to choose a program that aligns with their interests and career goals. It's essential for admissions representatives to be well-informed about the unique offerings of each school type to help prospective students make informed decisions about their education.

# ACCREDITATION AND LICENSING REQUIREMENTS

Explore the significance of accreditation and how it ensures that your chosen beauty school meets the industry's standards. We'll also cover the essential licensing requirements that every beauty professional in Florida must fulfill.

In Florida, it is possible to create a school without seeking accreditation. However, it's important to understand the implications of operating an unaccredited school, particularly in the context of beauty schools and career-oriented education.

Prospective school owners might choose not to pursue accreditation for various reasons, such as the desire for more flexibility in curriculum design, avoiding the costs associated with the accreditation process, or opting for a non-traditional approach to education.

**Here are some important points to consider about creating an unaccredited school in Florida:**

**Lack of Recognition and Credibility:**

Accreditation is an essential marker of quality and credibility for educational institutions. Without accreditation, the school's programs and certifications may not be recognized by employers, licensing boards, or other educational institutions. Graduates from unaccredited schools might face challenges when seeking employment or furthering their education.

**Student Financial Aid and Grants:**

Accredited schools are eligible for various forms of financial aid, including federal student loans and grants. Students attending unaccredited schools might not have access to these financial assistance options, making the cost of education a significant barrier.

**Limited Transferability of Credits:**

Students who attend an unaccredited school may find it challenging to transfer their credits to accredited institutions. This can hinder their ability to pursue further education at other schools or universities.

**Licensing and Approval:**

In Florida, specific career-oriented schools, including beauty schools, may require approval from the Florida Department of Education's Commission for

Independent Education (CIE). Even though accreditation is not mandatory, approval from CIE is necessary for certain career schools to operate legally.

**Public Perception:**

Accreditation provides an assurance of quality education to students and the general public. An unaccredited school might face skepticism and doubt about the quality of its programs and the legitimacy of its operations.

**State Regulations:**

Unaccredited schools in Florida are subject to state regulations and must comply with certain standards set by the Florida Department of Education. These standards ensure basic educational requirements and student protection.

For students considering attending an unaccredited school, it's crucial to thoroughly research the institution, its reputation, and the outcomes of previous students. Prospective students should carefully weigh the advantages and disadvantages of attending an unaccredited school and consider their long-term educational and career goals.

Admissions representatives should be transparent about their school's accreditation status and should provide accurate information about the potential impact of attending an unaccredited institution. They should also inform students about the school's approval from CIE and its compliance with relevant state regulations.

In Florida, CIE stands for the "Commission for Independent Education." It is a regulatory body under the Florida Department of Education responsible for overseeing and regulating private, postsecondary educational institutions, including career schools and colleges. The CIE's primary role is to ensure that these institutions meet the necessary standards and provide quality education to students while protecting their rights and interests.

## The Commission for Independent Education is responsible for:

### Licensing and Approval:

CIE reviews applications from private career schools and colleges seeking authorization to operate in Florida. It assesses the institution's compliance with state regulations, educational programs, faculty qualifications, facilities, and financial stability before granting approval.

### Oversight and Compliance:

Once approved, the CIE monitors the ongoing operations of these institutions to ensure that they continue to meet the state's educational and operational standards. Regular inspections and evaluations are conducted to maintain quality assurance.

### Consumer Protection:

The CIE is tasked with protecting student rights and interests. It investigates complaints from students and addresses issues related to deceptive practices, unfair treatment, or other violations of the state's rules and regulations.

### Maintaining a List of Approved Schools:

The CIE maintains a comprehensive list of approved career schools and colleges in Florida, which is accessible to the public. This list serves as a valuable resource for prospective students to verify the legitimacy and compliance of educational institutions.

**Enforcement of Regulations:**

If an institution fails to meet the required standards or violates state regulations, the CIE has the authority to take appropriate actions, which may include imposing fines, probation, suspension, or revocation of the institution's license.

It's crucial for students to verify that any career school or college they are considering attending is approved by the Florida Commission for Independent Education. Attending an approved school ensures that the institution meets the necessary standards and provides a level of assurance regarding the quality of education and the protection of student rights. Admissions representatives should be well-informed about the CIE's role and should guide prospective students through the approval process and compliance with state regulations.

Unaccredited school in Florida can work towards becoming an accredited school. Achieving accreditation is a significant milestone that requires dedication, time, and adherence to specific standards. Here's an overview of the process and milestones involved in transitioning from an unaccredited school to an accredited school in Florida:

**Research and Self-Assessment:**

The first step is for the school administration and stakeholders to conduct thorough research on accreditation agencies and their requirements. They should assess the school's current programs, policies, facilities, and operations to identify areas that need improvement to meet accreditation standards.

**Selecting an Accreditation Agency:**

The school must choose an appropriate accrediting agency that aligns with its educational mission and programs. In Florida, the main accrediting agency for beauty schools is the "National Accrediting Commission of Career Arts and Sciences" (NACCAS). However, other agencies might accredit schools in specific fields or specialties.

**Meeting Eligibility Criteria:**

Before applying for accreditation, the school must meet specific eligibility criteria set by the chosen accrediting agency. This may include a minimum period of operation, having a certain number of enrolled students, and maintaining a stable financial status.

**Completing a Self-Study Report:**

The school is required to conduct a comprehensive self-study, which involves an in-depth examination of all aspects of the institution. The self-study report serves as a foundation for the accreditation process and helps the school identify areas of improvement.

**Application and Pre-Visit Evaluation:**

The school submits an application for accreditation to the chosen accrediting agency. The agency then evaluates the application and may conduct a pre-visit to assess the school's readiness for the accreditation process.

**On-Site Evaluation and Review:**

The accrediting agency will conduct an on-site evaluation visit to the school. A team of evaluators will assess the institution's compliance with accreditation standards, review documentation, observe classes, and interview faculty, staff, and students.

## Accreditation Decision:

Based on the findings of the evaluation visit and review of the self-study report, the accrediting agency's commission will make a decision on whether to grant accreditation to the school.

## Implementation of Recommendations:

If the school receives conditional accreditation or is not granted accreditation initially, it must address any deficiencies or recommendations identified during the evaluation process. The school will work on improving areas that need development to meet accreditation standards.

## Maintaining Accreditation:

Once accredited, the school must continue to meet ongoing compliance and reporting requirements to maintain its accredited status. Regular evaluations and reports may be necessary to ensure the institution's continued adherence to accreditation standards.

Becoming an accredited school is a significant achievement that demonstrates the institution's commitment to providing quality education and meeting industry standards. It opens doors to various benefits, including federal financial aid options, increased credibility, and enhanced opportunities for students and graduates.

Becoming an accredited beauty school is a process that requires time, effort, and dedication. The timeline can vary depending on several factors, including the school's current status, the accrediting agency's requirements, and the school's ability to address any deficiencies in meeting accreditation standards. On average, the process to become an accredited beauty school can take anywhere from 1 to 3 years or even longer. Here's a rough breakdown of the timeline:

**Research and Preparatory Phase (6 months - 1 year):**

During this phase, the school conducts research on various accrediting agencies and their requirements. They also assess their current programs, facilities, and operations to identify areas that need improvement to meet accreditation standards.

**Selection of Accrediting Agency (1 - 3 months):**

Choosing the appropriate accrediting agency that aligns with the school's educational mission and programs may take some time. The school must thoroughly review the agency's standards and processes before making a decision.

**Meeting Eligibility Criteria (Varies):**

The time taken to meet the eligibility criteria set by the accrediting agency can vary depending on the school's current status. Some criteria, such as minimum years of operation, financial stability, and student enrollment numbers, may need to be fulfilled before the official application can be made.

**Self-Study and Documentation (6 - 12 months):**

Preparing the self-study report and gathering all the necessary documentation for the accreditation application can be a time-consuming process. The school must thoroughly analyze its operations, policies, and educational outcomes.

## Accreditation Application (1 - 3 months):

The actual application process involves submitting the self-study report and necessary documentation to the accrediting agency. This process usually takes a few months for the agency to review the application and decide whether to proceed with an on-site evaluation.

## On-Site Evaluation (1 - 2 months):

The on-site evaluation visit is conducted by a team of evaluators from the accrediting agency. They assess the school's compliance with accreditation standards, interview faculty, staff, and students, and observe classes and facilities.

## Accreditation Decision (1 - 3 months):

After the on-site evaluation, the accrediting agency's commission reviews the findings and makes a decision on whether to grant accreditation to the school. This process can take a few months to finalize.

## Implementation of Recommendations (Varies):

If the school receives conditional accreditation or is not granted accreditation initially, it must address any deficiencies or recommendations identified during the evaluation process. This can add extra time to the overall process.

It's important to note that the timeline provided above is a rough estimate, and the actual duration can vary based on the specific circumstances of each beauty school and the accrediting agency involved. Admissions representatives should work closely with school administrators and the accrediting agency to ensure a smooth and efficient accreditation process.

# SPECIALIZATIONS AND PROGRAMS

Uncover the array of specialized beauty programs available in Florida. Whether you dream of becoming a skilled makeup artist, a proficient hairstylist, or a skincare expert, we'll guide you through the diverse educational pathways you can pursue.

**Specializations and Programs Offered:**
**Cosmetology Program:**

The Cosmetology Program is a comprehensive course that covers a wide range of beauty services, including hair care, skincare, nail care, and makeup artistry. Students learn fundamental and advanced techniques in hair cutting, coloring, styling, chemical treatments, facials, waxing, and makeup application. The program aims to prepare students to become well-rounded beauty professionals capable of meeting diverse client needs.

**Esthetics Program:**

The Esthetics Program focuses specifically on skincare and facial treatments. Students learn various skincare techniques, such as facials, exfoliation, extractions, and chemical peels. They also gain expertise in analyzing different skin types, identifying specific skin concerns, and providing personalized skincare solutions to clients.

## Barbering Program:

The Barbering Program concentrates on men's grooming and haircare. Students acquire skills in traditional and contemporary barbering techniques, including haircutting, shaving, beard and mustache grooming, and hairstyling for men. The curriculum often includes training in scalp and facial treatments.

## Nail Technology Program:

The Nail Technology Program focuses on the art of nail care and design. Students learn the intricacies of manicures, pedicures, nail art, and various nail enhancement techniques, such as acrylics, gels, and nail extensions. Emphasis is placed on maintaining nail health, practicing sanitation, and ensuring the overall well-being of clients' nails.

## Makeup Artistry Program:

The Makeup Artistry Program is designed to train students in the art and application of makeup. Students learn various makeup styles, ranging from natural and bridal makeup to high-fashion and special effects makeup. The curriculum includes instruction in color theory, contouring, highlighting, and using makeup to enhance facial features and create different looks.

## Permanent Makeup Program:

The Permanent Makeup Program provides specialized training in micro-pigmentation techniques. Students learn to apply permanent makeup for eyebrows, eyeliner, lip color, and other facial enhancements. The curriculum emphasizes the safe use of pigment and proper sterilization practices to ensure client safety.

**Salon Management Program:**

The Salon Management Program is designed for students interested in pursuing careers in salon ownership or management. The curriculum covers business and management principles, marketing strategies, financial planning, and human resources management specific to the beauty industry. This program equips students with the knowledge and skills needed to run a successful salon business.

**Advanced Specializations:**

Some beauty schools offer additional advanced specializations or continuing education programs for licensed professionals. These may include advanced courses in hair coloring and styling techniques, advanced skincare treatments, advanced nail artistry, or certification courses in specific beauty product lines.

Each beauty school may offer a combination of these programs tailored to meet the needs and preferences of their students. Admissions representatives should be well-versed in the programs offered by their school and provide detailed information to prospective students, including program duration, curriculum content, hands-on training opportunities, and potential career pathways after completion.

# PREPARING FOR BEAUTY SCHOOL ADMISSION

## IDENTIFYING YOUR CAREER GOALS

Reflect on your personal goals and aspirations within the beauty industry. By understanding your passions, strengths, and interests, you can align your career objectives with the right beauty school program.

**Self-Reflection and Interests:**

One of the first steps in identifying career goals is self-reflection. Prospective students should ask themselves what aspects of the beauty industry they are most passionate about. Are they drawn to hairstyling, makeup artistry, skincare, nail technology, or a combination of these? Identifying their interests will help them narrow down their career options.

**Researching Beauty Specializations:**

Students should research different beauty specializations to gain a deeper understanding of each field's opportunities and requirements. They can explore the day-to-day tasks, work environments, potential income, and career growth prospects for professionals in each area.

**Personal Skills and Strengths:**

Identifying personal skills and strengths can guide students toward the beauty specialization that aligns with their natural abilities. For example, those with strong artistic skills might excel in makeup artistry, while individuals with excellent communication and people skills may thrive in a customer-facing role like cosmetology.

**Career Aspirations and Long-Term Goals:**

Students should envision their long-term career aspirations in the beauty industry. Do they see themselves working as salon owners, freelance artists, or educators? Understanding their ultimate goals will help them make informed decisions about the educational path to pursue.

**Desired Work Environment:**

Students should consider the type of work environment that appeals to them. Some may prefer the fast-paced atmosphere of a salon or spa, while others might enjoy the creativity and flexibility of freelancing or working in the entertainment industry.

**Salary Expectations and Job Market:**

Researching salary expectations and the job market for their chosen specialization is crucial. Prospective students should have a realistic understanding of potential income levels and the demand for professionals in their desired field.

**Work-Life Balance and Flexibility:**

Students should assess their desired work-life balance and flexibility. Certain beauty careers may involve irregular hours or require travel, while others offer more structured schedules.

**Long-Term Commitment:**

Entering the beauty industry requires dedication and passion. Students should consider whether they see themselves committed to their chosen specialization for the long term and if it aligns with their personal values and goals.

**Seeking Guidance:**

Seeking guidance from career counselors, industry professionals, and current students or graduates can be invaluable. Speaking with people who have firsthand experience in the beauty industry can provide insights and advice.

**Setting Short-Term and Long-Term Goals:**

Finally, students should set specific short-term and long-term goals to achieve their career aspirations. These goals may include enrolling in a specific beauty school program, gaining hands-on experience through internships, or obtaining industry certifications.

By carefully considering these aspects and asking relevant questions, prospective beauty school students can gain clarity on their career goals and choose a program that aligns with their passions and aspirations. Admissions representatives can assist students in this process by providing comprehensive information about different beauty specializations, potential career pathways, and the educational offerings available at their school.

# ACADEMIC REQUIREMENTS AND PREREQUISITES

Get an insight into the academic prerequisites necessary for beauty school admission. Whether you're a recent high school graduate or a career changer, we'll provide guidance on meeting the academic criteria.

**Academic Requirements and Prerequisites:**

**High School Diploma or Equivalent:**

One of the most common academic requirements for beauty school admission is a high school diploma or its equivalent, such as a General Educational Development (GED) certificate. Admissions representatives will typically request official documentation or transcripts to verify this qualification.

**Minimum Age Requirement:**

Some beauty schools may have a minimum age requirement for enrollment. In Florida, the minimum age to attend beauty school is typically 16 years old. However, age requirements can vary among institutions, so students should check with the specific school they are interested in.

**Language Proficiency:**

Beauty school instruction is often conducted in English, so students should demonstrate proficiency in the language. Depending on the school's policy, applicants may need to provide proof of language proficiency through standardized tests or language assessment exams.

**Basic Math and English Skills:**

Proficiency in basic math and English skills is essential for beauty school programs. Students should be able to perform measurements, calculations, and conversions related to salon operations, as well as communicate effectively with clients and colleagues.

**Health and Safety Requirements:**

Some beauty schools may have specific health and safety requirements for admission. This may include completing health forms, providing immunization records, or passing a physical examination to ensure that students can safely participate in hands-on training.

**Specific Program Prerequisites:**

Certain beauty school programs may have additional prerequisites or recommended coursework for admission. For example, advanced programs like esthetics or makeup artistry might require applicants to complete a basic cosmetology program or have relevant industry experience.

**Application Fee:**

Beauty schools typically require applicants to pay an application fee when submitting their application. This fee covers the administrative costs of processing the application.

**Interview or Assessment:**

Some beauty schools may require applicants to undergo an interview or skills assessment as part of the admission process. The interview helps the school evaluate the applicant's passion for the beauty industry, while the assessment may test basic skills relevant to the chosen program.

**Transfer Credit Evaluation (for Transfer Students):**

For transfer students who have completed coursework at other institutions, beauty schools may evaluate their transcripts to determine if any credits can be transferred. This process helps determine the student's progress in meeting program requirements.

Admissions representatives should clearly communicate the specific academic requirements and prerequisites for each beauty school program to prospective students. Providing a checklist of required documents and a step-by-step guide to the application process can help students navigate the admission process smoothly. Additionally, admissions representatives should be available to answer any questions or concerns applicants may have regarding academic requirements and prerequisites.

# ESSENTIAL SKILLS AND TRAITS FOR BEAUTY PROFESSIONALS

Discover the traits and skills that successful beauty professionals possess. Learn how cultivating creativity, communication, and client service skills will enhance your potential for a thriving career in the beauty industry.

**Essential Skills and Traits for Beauty Professionals:**

**Creativity and Artistic Vision:**

Beauty professionals need a strong sense of creativity and artistic vision to create unique and aesthetically pleasing looks for their clients. They should be able to conceptualize and execute different styles, colors, and designs to enhance their clients' appearance.

**Attention to Detail:**

Precision and attention to detail are crucial in the beauty industry. Whether it's performing intricate nail art, precise makeup application, or meticulous hair cutting, beauty professionals must pay close attention to every detail to achieve the desired results.

**Communication and Interpersonal Skills:**

Effective communication is essential for understanding clients' needs and preferences. Beauty professionals should be good listeners, able to ask relevant questions, and communicate clearly to ensure clients' expectations are met. Strong interpersonal skills help create a positive and comfortable experience for clients.

**Customer Service Skills:**

Providing exceptional customer service is key to building a loyal client base. Beauty professionals should be friendly, approachable, and attentive, ensuring that clients feel valued and well-cared for throughout their salon or spa visit.

**Time Management:**

The beauty industry often involves working with multiple clients throughout the day. Time management skills are crucial for organizing appointments efficiently, ensuring clients are served promptly, and maintaining a smooth flow in the salon or spa.

**Stamina and Physical Endurance:**

Beauty professionals spend long hours on their feet and may perform repetitive tasks throughout the day. Physical endurance and stamina are necessary to handle the demands of the profession and maintain energy levels during busy working hours.

**Adaptability and Flexibility:**

The beauty industry is dynamic, and trends and client preferences can change rapidly. Beauty professionals should be adaptable and willing to learn new techniques and stay updated with industry trends to meet the evolving needs of their clients.

**Business and Marketing Skills:**

For beauty professionals who aspire to run their own salons or freelance businesses, basic business and marketing skills are essential. This includes knowledge of budgeting, pricing, inventory management, and effective marketing strategies to attract and retain clients.

**Commitment to Hygiene and Sanitation:**

Maintaining a clean and sanitary work environment is paramount in the beauty industry. Beauty professionals must adhere to strict hygiene and sanitation practices to ensure the safety and well-being of their clients.

**Emotional Intelligence and Empathy:**

Beauty professionals often develop close relationships with their clients. Emotional intelligence and empathy help them understand and connect with clients on a deeper level, making the overall experience more enjoyable and satisfying for the clients.

**Continuous Learning and Professional Development:**

The beauty industry is constantly evolving, and successful beauty professionals embrace lifelong learning and professional development. They attend workshops, seminars, and training programs to stay updated with the latest techniques, products, and technologies.

Admissions representatives should emphasize these essential skills and traits to prospective students, highlighting their importance in building a successful and rewarding career in the beauty industry. By nurturing and developing these qualities, aspiring beauty professionals can excel in their chosen specialization and leave a positive impact on their clients.

# EXPLORING BEAUTY SCHOOL OPTIONS

## RESEARCHING DIFFERENT BEAUTY SCHOOLS IN FLORIDA

Gain valuable tips on researching beauty schools in Florida. From evaluating their reputations to examining their facilities and faculty, we'll help you make an informed decision when choosing the right school for your needs.

Researching different beauty schools in Florida is a crucial step in the process of pursuing your beauty education. Making an informed decision about the right school for your needs can greatly impact your learning experience and future career opportunities. Here are some key aspects to consider when researching beauty schools in Florida:

**Accreditation and Licensing:**

Ensure that the beauty school you are considering is accredited by the relevant state and national accrediting bodies. Accreditation indicates that the school meets specific educational standards and can provide quality education. Additionally, verify that the school's programs meet the licensing requirements set by the Florida Department of Business and Professional Regulation (DBPR).

**Reputation and Reviews:**

Research the school's reputation by checking online reviews, testimonials from current and past students, and industry professionals. A reputable beauty school is more likely to offer a comprehensive curriculum, experienced instructors, and excellent facilities.

**Program Offerings:**

Explore the different beauty programs offered by each school and determine if they align with your career goals and interests. Look for schools that provide specialized programs and certifications in areas such as cosmetology, esthetics, makeup artistry, barbering, nail technology, and more.

**Facilities and Resources:**

Visit the school's campus or take virtual tours to examine its facilities and resources. A well-equipped beauty school with modern equipment and a conducive learning environment can enhance your education and practical training.

**Faculty Qualifications:**

Research the qualifications and experience of the school's faculty members. Experienced and knowledgeable instructors can provide valuable insights and mentorship, leading to a more enriching learning experience.

## Job Placement and Alumni Success:

Inquire about the school's job placement assistance and track record of alumni success. A school that actively helps graduates find employment opportunities in the beauty industry can significantly impact your post-graduation prospects.

## Class Size and Student Support:

Consider the class sizes and student-to-faculty ratios. Smaller class sizes often mean more individualized attention and support from instructors, leading to a better learning experience.

## Financial Aid and Tuition Costs:

Research the school's tuition fees and available financial aid options. A school that offers scholarships, grants, or flexible payment plans can ease the financial burden of your education.

## Location and Commute:

Consider the school's location and how convenient it is for you to commute. Proximity to public transportation and other amenities may be important factors to consider.

## Accommodations for Special Needs:

If you have specific accommodation needs, such as accessibility requirements or language support, ensure that the school can meet these needs.

By thoroughly researching different beauty schools in Florida, you can make an informed decision that aligns with your career aspirations and educational goals. Don't hesitate to reach out to admissions representatives, ask questions, and gather as much information as possible before making your final choice. Remember that investing time and effort in researching your beauty school can lead to a rewarding and successful journey in the beauty industry.

# VISITING CAMPUSES AND FACILITIES

Embark on campus visits to get a firsthand experience of the beauty school environment. This chapter provides insights on what to look for during your campus tour and how to ask the right questions.

Visiting campuses and facilities is an essential part of the decision-making process when choosing a beauty school. A campus visit provides you with a firsthand experience of the environment, atmosphere, and facilities, allowing you to assess whether the school aligns with your educational needs and preferences. Here are some key insights on what to look for during your campus tour and how to ask the right questions:

**Facility Tour:**

Take a comprehensive tour of the beauty school's facilities. Pay attention to the layout and organization of classrooms, labs, and practical training areas. Check if the spaces are clean, well-maintained, and equipped with modern tools and equipment relevant to your chosen specialization.

**Classroom and Lab Environment:**

Observe the classroom and lab environment. A conducive learning space should be comfortable, well-lit, and conducive to focused learning. Assess the availability of tools, materials, and products needed for hands-on training.

**Instructor Interaction:**

During the campus visit, try to interact with the instructors and faculty members. Ask about their teaching approaches, industry experience, and their commitment to student success. Engaging with instructors will give you a sense of the support and mentorship you can expect during your education.

**Student-to-Faculty Ratio:**

Inquire about the student-to-faculty ratio. A lower ratio allows for more personalized attention and support from instructors, which can enhance your learning experience.

**Student Services and Support:**

Learn about the student services and support offered by the school. Services such as academic advising, career counseling, and job placement assistance can be valuable resources to help you succeed in your beauty school journey and beyond.

**Practical Training Opportunities:**

Understand the extent of practical training opportunities the school offers. Practical experience is critical in the beauty industry, so ensure that the school provides ample hands-on training through client services or simulated scenarios.

**Industry Partnerships and Guest Speakers:**

Inquire about the school's industry partnerships and any guest speakers or professionals who visit the campus. Exposure to industry experts and guest speakers can provide valuable insights and networking opportunities.

**Student Life and Culture:**

Take note of the overall student life and culture on campus. Observe how students interact with one another and the school community. A positive and supportive campus environment can contribute to a more enriching learning experience.

**Financial Aid and Scholarships:** Ask about available financial aid options, scholarships, and tuition payment plans. Understanding the financial support available can help you plan for the cost of your education.

**Career Services and Alumni Success:**

Inquire about the school's career services and track record of alumni success. Learn about the resources available to assist graduates in finding employment opportunities in the beauty industry.

Asking the right questions during your campus visit can provide you with valuable insights and help you make an informed decision about the best beauty school for your needs and aspirations. Remember to trust your instincts and choose a school that resonates with your goals and values, ultimately setting you on the path to a successful and fulfilling career in the beauty industry.

# COMPARING TUITION AND FINANCIAL AID OPTIONS

Learn about the financial aspects of attending beauty school. We'll guide you through understanding tuition costs, available financial aid programs, and scholarship opportunities to ease the burden of funding your education.

**Comparing Tuition and Financial Aid Options:**

**Tuition Costs:**

Tuition costs can vary significantly among beauty schools, depending on the program's duration, location, and reputation. Prospective students should request detailed information about the total cost of their chosen program, including tuition fees, registration fees, and any additional expenses for books, supplies, and uniforms.

**Financial Aid Programs:**

Beauty schools often participate in various federal and state financial aid programs to assist eligible students in funding their education. Some common financial aid options include:

**Federal Pell Grant:**

This grant provides need-based financial assistance to undergraduate students pursuing their first degree or a qualifying certificate program. The grant amount depends on the student's financial need, cost of attendance, and enrollment status.

**Federal Direct Loans:**

These are low-interest loans provided by the U.S. Department of Education to eligible students and parents. Subsidized loans do not accrue interest while the student is in school, while unsubsidized loans do. Repayment typically begins after graduation.

**Federal Work-Study Program:**

This program provides part-time job opportunities for students with financial need, allowing them to earn money to help cover educational expenses.

State Grants and Scholarships: Many states offer grants and scholarships specifically for students attending in-state beauty schools. These awards are often based on academic achievement, financial need, or specific career goals.

**School-Specific Scholarships and Grants:**

Beauty schools may offer their own scholarships and grants to eligible students. These awards can be merit-based, need-based, or geared toward students pursuing specific specializations within the beauty industry. Admissions representatives should inform students about the availability of such school-specific financial aid options.

**Private Loans:**

In addition to federal loans, some students may opt for private loans from banks or lending institutions to cover tuition costs. Private loans often have higher interest rates and may require a co-signer, so students should carefully consider the terms before choosing this option.

**Payment Plans:**

Many beauty schools offer flexible payment plans, allowing students to spread their tuition costs over several months. This can help ease the financial burden and make paying for education more manageable.

**Budgeting and Financial Planning:**

Admissions representatives can guide prospective students in creating a budget and financial plan for their beauty school education. This involves estimating total costs, exploring available financial aid options, and assessing personal financial resources.

**Financial Aid Application Process:**

Admissions representatives should provide clear instructions on how to apply for financial aid, including the Free Application for Federal Student Aid (FAFSA) for federal assistance. They should inform students about deadlines, required documents, and any additional forms or applications needed for school-specific aid.

By assisting students in comparing tuition costs and exploring various financial aid options, admissions representatives can empower them to make informed decisions about funding their beauty school education. Encouraging financial literacy and responsible borrowing ensures that students have the necessary resources to pursue their career goals in the beauty industry without unnecessary financial strain.

# THE APPLICATION PROCESS

## APPLICATION DEADLINES AND KEY DATES

Stay on top of the application process by understanding important deadlines and key dates for submission. We'll outline essential timelines to help you submit your application promptly and avoid missing any crucial steps.

**Application Deadlines and Key Dates:**

**Early Admission Deadlines:**

Some beauty schools may offer early admission options for prospective students who apply before a specific date. Early admission can provide certain advantages, such as priority consideration for financial aid, housing options, or enrollment in high-demand programs. Admissions representatives should inform students about the benefits and deadlines for early admission.

**Regular Admission Deadlines:**

Regular admission deadlines are the standard application deadlines for most beauty schools. These deadlines typically fall several months before the start of the program, allowing sufficient time for processing applications, conducting interviews (if required), and notifying accepted students.

**Rolling Admissions:**

Some beauty schools may have rolling admissions, meaning they review and accept applications as they are received, rather than waiting for a specific deadline. In such cases, it is advantageous for students to apply early to secure their spot in the program.

**Start Dates and Program Durations:**

Admissions representatives should provide information on the specific start dates for each beauty school program and the program's duration. This enables students to plan their schedules and commitments accordingly.

**Financial Aid Application Deadlines:**

Financial aid programs, such as the Free Application for Federal Student Aid (FAFSA), have specific deadlines for application submission. Admissions representatives should inform students about these deadlines to ensure they have ample time to complete the necessary paperwork and be considered for financial assistance.

**Housing and Accommodation Deadlines:**

For students considering relocating or attending beauty schools in different cities, it is essential to be aware of housing and accommodation deadlines. Many schools have limited on-campus housing options or partnerships with off-campus housing providers, and early planning can help secure suitable accommodations.

## Orientation and Registration Dates:

Orientation and registration dates are important milestones for accepted students. These sessions provide essential information about the school, its facilities, policies, and academic requirements. Admissions representatives should communicate these dates to ensure students can participate in these crucial events.

## Enrollment Deposit Deadlines:

After acceptance, students may be required to submit an enrollment deposit to secure their spot in the program. Admissions representatives should clearly communicate the amount of the deposit, the deadline for submission, and any refund policies.

## Document Submission Deadlines:

Students may need to submit additional documents, such as official transcripts, test scores, letters of recommendation, or health forms. Admissions representatives should provide a checklist of required documents and their respective deadlines to ensure a complete application.

## Transfer Credit Evaluation Deadlines:

If a student is transferring credits from another institution, there may be specific deadlines for submitting transcripts for evaluation. This process determines which credits can be transferred and applied to the beauty school program.

By providing comprehensive information about application deadlines and key dates, admissions representatives can support students in completing their applications on time and securing a smooth transition into their beauty school journey. Clear communication and timely reminders about important dates are crucial in ensuring that students have a positive and stress-free application experience.

# REQUIRED DOCUMENTS AND SUPPORTING MATERIALS

Gather the necessary documents and supporting materials required for your beauty school application. From transcripts and letters of recommendation to portfolio samples, we'll guide you through preparing a comprehensive application package.

**Required Documents and Supporting Materials:**
**Application Form:**

The application form is the initial document that students need to complete when applying to a beauty school. It provides basic personal information, contact details, and the desired program of study.

**High School Diploma or Equivalent:**

A copy of the student's high school diploma or equivalent (such as a GED certificate) is typically required as proof of educational attainment.

## Transcripts:

Official high school transcripts are often required to verify the student's academic history and performance. For transfer students, transcripts from any previous postsecondary education should also be provided for credit evaluation.

## Letters of Recommendation:

Some beauty schools may request letters of recommendation from teachers, counselors, or other individuals who can speak to the student's character, work ethic, and potential for success in the beauty industry.

## Personal Statement or Essay:

A personal statement or essay is an opportunity for students to express their passion for the beauty industry, their career aspirations, and why they believe they are a good fit for the program.

## Resume or Portfolio:

A resume or portfolio is particularly relevant for students pursuing specialized programs like makeup artistry or advanced hairstyling. It showcases their previous work, experience, and any relevant certifications or achievements.

## Proof of Identity and Citizenship:

Students may need to provide proof of identity, such as a government-issued photo ID, and proof of citizenship or residency, such as a birth certificate or passport.

## Financial Aid Documents:

For students applying for financial aid, the necessary documents include the Free Application for Federal

Student Aid (FAFSA) and any other forms specific to the school's financial aid process.

**Health and Immunization Records:**

Some beauty schools may require health and immunization records to ensure that students are physically capable of participating in hands-on training and to protect the health of the school community.

**English Language Proficiency (if applicable):**

For international students or students whose first language is not English, proof of English language proficiency, such as TOEFL or IELTS scores, may be required.

**Interview or Audition Materials (if applicable):**

Some beauty schools may require an interview or audition as part of the application process, particularly for specialized programs. Students should be prepared with any required materials or portfolios for these evaluations.

**Application Fee:**

An application fee is a common requirement when submitting an application. This fee covers administrative costs associated with processing the application.

Admissions representatives should provide a clear and detailed checklist of the required documents and supporting materials for each beauty school program. This information helps students prepare a complete and organized application package and ensures a smooth and efficient application process. Additionally, admissions representatives should be available to answer any questions and provide guidance on gathering and submitting the necessary documents.

# ADMISSIONS INTERVIEWS AND ASSESSMENTS

## PREPARING FOR ADMISSIONS INTERVIEWS

Ace your beauty school admissions interviews with confidence. Learn how to present yourself professionally, answer common interview questions, and demonstrate your dedication to the beauty profession.

Preparing for admissions interviews is a critical step in the beauty school application process. The interview is an opportunity for you to showcase your passion for the beauty profession and demonstrate why you are the right fit for the school.

Here are some key insights on how to excel in your beauty school admissions interviews:

**Professional Appearance:**

Dress professionally and groom yourself neatly for the interview. Your appearance should reflect your understanding of the beauty industry's emphasis on personal presentation and professionalism.

**Research the School:**

Familiarize yourself with the beauty school's programs, values, and achievements. Understanding the school's unique offerings will enable you to tailor your responses and show genuine interest in their educational offerings.

**Practice Common Interview Questions:**

Practice answering common interview questions, such as why you want to pursue a career in the beauty industry, your career goals, and how the school aligns with your aspirations. Rehearsing your responses will help you articulate your thoughts clearly during the actual interview.

**Demonstrate Passion and Dedication:**

Express your passion for the beauty profession and your commitment to honing your skills. Admissions representatives want to see that you are genuinely enthusiastic about embarking on this career path.

**Highlight Relevant Experience:**

If you have any prior experience in the beauty industry, such as part-time work, volunteer opportunities, or creative projects, be sure to highlight them during the interview. This demonstrates your initiative and hands-on approach to learning.

**Discuss Your Strengths and Goals:**

Share your strengths and how they can contribute to your success in beauty school. Also, discuss your short-term and long-term career goals to illustrate your determination and vision for the future.

**Ask Questions:**

Prepare thoughtful questions to ask the admissions representatives. Inquiring about the school's support services, hands-on training opportunities, and industry partnerships shows your interest in making an informed decision.

**Confidence and Positive Attitude:**

Approach the interview with confidence and a positive attitude. Smile, maintain eye contact, and engage with the interviewer in a friendly and enthusiastic manner.

**Be Yourself:**

Be authentic and true to yourself during the interview. Admissions representatives are looking for individuals who will contribute positively to the school's community and culture.

**Follow-Up:**

After the interview, consider sending a thank-you note or email to express your appreciation for the opportunity. This simple gesture can leave a positive impression and reinforce your interest in attending the beauty school.

By preparing thoroughly for your admissions interviews, you can showcase your passion, dedication, and suitability for a career in the beauty industry. The interview is your chance to stand out and make a lasting impression, so approach it with confidence and enthusiasm. Remember, admissions representatives want to see your potential and commitment to succeed in beauty school and beyond.

# DEMONSTRATING YOUR PASSION AND COMMITMENT

Discover the art of conveying your genuine passion for beauty during admissions interviews. Showcase your enthusiasm, drive, and commitment to learning as you embark on this exciting educational journey.

# UNDERSTANDING FINANCIAL AID AND SCHOLARSHIPS

## AVAILABLE FINANCIAL AID PROGRAMS IN FLORIDA

Explore the range of financial aid options available to beauty school students in Florida. From federal grants to state-specific programs, we'll guide you through the financial support options at your disposal.

In Florida, various financial aid programs are available to help students pursue their education, including beauty school programs. These programs are designed to provide financial assistance to eligible students, making education more accessible and affordable.

Here are some of the key financial aid programs available in Florida:

**Federal Pell Grant:**

The Federal Pell Grant is a need-based grant offered by the U.S. Department of Education. Eligibility is determined based on the student's financial need, cost of attendance, and enrollment status. The grant does not need to be repaid and can be used to cover educational expenses, including tuition, books, and supplies.

**Federal Direct Loans:**

Federal Direct Loans are low-interest loans provided by the U.S. Department of Education. There are two types of federal direct loans: subsidized and unsubsidized. Subsidized loans are need-based, and the government pays the interest while the student is in school. Unsubsidized loans are available to all eligible students, and interest accrues while the student is in school. Repayment typically begins after graduation.

**Federal Work-Study Program:**

The Federal Work-Study Program provides part-time job opportunities for students with financial need. Eligible students can work on-campus or off-campus in positions related to their course of study or community service. The income earned helps cover educational expenses.

**Florida Student Assistance Grant (FSAG):**

The FSAG is a need-based grant offered by the state of Florida. It provides financial assistance to undergraduate students attending eligible institutions in Florida. Eligibility is based on financial need, and the grant amount varies depending on available funding.

## Bright Futures Scholarship Program:

The Bright Futures Scholarship Program is a merit-based scholarship program funded by the Florida Lottery. It offers three scholarship levels: Florida Academic Scholars (FAS), Florida Medallion Scholars (FMS), and Florida Gold Seal Vocational Scholars (GSV). Eligibility is determined by academic achievement, community service, and specific coursework completed in high school.

## Florida Student Scholarship and Grant Programs:

Florida offers various other scholarship and grant programs to support students pursuing higher education. These include the Access to Better Learning and Education (ABLE) Grant, Florida Resident Access Grant (FRAG), and Rosewood Family Scholarship, among others.

## Florida Prepaid College Program:

The Florida Prepaid College Program allows families to prepay tuition and fees for Florida colleges and universities, including some beauty schools. This program offers flexible payment options and helps families save for future educational expenses.

## CareerSource Florida Scholarships:

CareerSource Florida provides workforce education and training scholarships to eligible individuals seeking employment-focused education, including beauty school programs. These scholarships aim to support students in gaining skills that align with industry demands.

Eligibility and award amounts for these financial aid programs vary based on factors such as income, enrollment status, and academic achievements. Students interested in financial aid should complete the Free Application for Federal Student Aid (FAFSA) to determine their eligibility for federal and state financial aid programs. Additionally, students should check with their beauty school's financial aid office to explore specific scholarship and grant opportunities offered by the school itself.

# SCHOLARSHIPS AND GRANTS FOR BEAUTY SCHOOL STUDENTS

Learn about scholarships and grants specifically tailored for aspiring beauty professionals. We'll highlight organizations and institutions offering financial assistance to help you pursue your dreams without financial constraints.

Scholarships and grants are valuable financial aid options that can significantly reduce the financial burden of attending beauty school. Here are some specific scholarships and grants available for beauty school students:

**Cosmetology Scholarships:**

Several organizations and beauty schools offer cosmetology scholarships specifically for students pursuing careers in cosmetology, including hairdressing, nail technology, and esthetics. These scholarships may be merit-based, need-based, or awarded based on specific criteria such as creativity, leadership, or community involvement.

**Makeup Artistry Scholarships:**

Makeup artistry scholarships are geared towards students interested in makeup application and the beauty industry's creative aspects. These scholarships may cover the cost of makeup kits, specialized courses, or overall tuition.

**Barbering Scholarships:**

Barbering scholarships are available for students interested in pursuing careers in men's grooming and hairstyling. These scholarships may be offered by barbering schools, industry associations, or private organizations.

**Esthetics and Skincare Scholarships:**

Esthetics scholarships are designed for students interested in skincare and facial treatments. These scholarships may cover tuition, supplies, or advanced training in esthetician programs.

**Nail Technology Scholarships:**

Nail technology scholarships are available for students focused on nail care and design. These scholarships can help cover the costs of nail technology programs and supplies.

**Underrepresented Community Scholarships:**

Some scholarships aim to promote diversity and inclusion in the beauty industry. These scholarships may be targeted towards students from underrepresented communities, including racial and ethnic minorities or LGBTQ+ individuals.

**Beauty School-specific Scholarships:**

Many beauty schools offer their own scholarships and grants to attract talented students and support their education. These scholarships may be based on academic achievement, financial need, or dedication to the beauty industry.

**Industry Association Scholarships:**

Professional beauty industry associations, such as the Professional Beauty Association (PBA) and the American Association of Cosmetology Schools (AACS), offer scholarships to support aspiring beauty professionals. These scholarships often require membership in the respective association.

**Community Foundation Scholarships:**

Community foundations may offer scholarships to students pursuing education in various fields, including beauty school programs. Students should research local community foundations to explore available opportunities.

**State and Federal Grants:**

In addition to scholarships, beauty school students may be eligible for state and federal grants, such as the Federal Pell Grant or state-specific grants like the Florida Student Assistance Grant (FSAG). These grants are need-based and do not require repayment.

To access these scholarships and grants, students should carefully review the eligibility criteria, application deadlines, and required documentation for each opportunity. Admissions representatives can provide guidance on available financial aid options and assist students in applying for scholarships and grants to help fund their beauty school education.

# BUDGETING FOR YOUR BEAUTY SCHOOL EDUCATION

Create a realistic budget for your beauty school education, factoring in tuition, books, supplies, and living expenses. Our expert tips will help you manage your finances wisely throughout your academic journey.

As admission representatives, your role is not only to guide potential students through the application process but also to assist them in understanding the financial aspects of their beauty school education. Here's how you can help potential students create a helpful budget:

**Tuition and Fees:**

Provide detailed information about the total cost of tuition and fees for the specific beauty school program the student is interested in. Break down the expenses, including registration fees, textbooks, and supplies, so they have a clear picture of the financial commitment.

**Financial Aid Options:**

Inform potential students about the various financial aid programs available, such as scholarships, grants, and loans. Explain the eligibility criteria and application process for each program to help them explore funding opportunities.

**Personal Budgeting:**

Encourage students to assess their personal finances and create a budget that factors in both income and expenses. Help them understand how to manage their finances efficiently during their time in beauty school.

**Living Expenses:**

Discuss living expenses, including housing, transportation, and meals. Provide information on affordable housing options near the beauty school and public transportation routes.

**Part-Time Work Opportunities:**

Inform students about part-time job opportunities on or off-campus, such as work-study programs or positions in the beauty industry. Emphasize the importance of balancing work commitments with academic responsibilities.

**Payment Plans:**

Explain any payment plan options offered by the beauty school, allowing students to spread their tuition payments over several months. This can make budgeting more manageable.

**Avoiding Unnecessary Expenses:**

Advise students on how to avoid unnecessary expenses and prioritize spending on essentials. Encourage them to be mindful of discretionary spending, such as entertainment and dining out.

**Textbook and Supplies Savings:**

Suggest cost-saving strategies, such as purchasing used textbooks or sharing supplies with classmates. Some beauty schools may also offer discounted supplies or provide certain items as part of the program.

**Financial Literacy Workshops:**

Organize financial literacy workshops or information sessions to educate potential students about budgeting, managing debt, and building credit responsibly.

**Long-Term Financial Planning:**

Help students understand the long-term implications of their beauty school investment. Discuss potential career pathways, salary expectations, and loan repayment strategies to ensure they make informed financial decisions.

# CONVINCING POTENTIAL STUDENTS TO MAKE A HELPFUL BUDGET:

**Empathy and Understanding:**

Demonstrate empathy and understanding of the financial concerns potential students may have. Show them that you are there to support them throughout the budgeting process.

**Highlighting Financial Aid Options:**

Emphasize the various financial aid programs available to ease their financial burden. Showcase success stories of previous students who received financial assistance and excelled in their beauty school journey.

**Personalized Approach:**

Tailor your budgeting advice to each student's unique financial situation. Provide individualized guidance based on their income, expenses, and specific financial goals.

**Success Stories and Testimonials:**

Share success stories and testimonials from alumni who successfully managed their finances during beauty school and now have thriving careers in the industry.

**Transparency and Honesty:**

Be transparent about the costs involved and any potential challenges they might face. Honesty builds trust and helps students feel confident in their financial decisions.

**Offering Resources:**

Provide resources, such as budgeting worksheets, financial planning tools, and information on scholarships and grants, to help students take control of their financial journey.

**Stress on the Value of Education:**

Remind students that investing in their education is an investment in their future. A beauty school education can open doors to exciting career opportunities and personal growth.

By proactively addressing potential financial concerns and offering support in budgeting, admission representatives can help potential students feel confident and empowered to pursue their beauty school education without unnecessary financial stress.

# NAVIGATING LICENSING AND CERTIFICATION

## FLORIDA LICENSING REQUIREMENTS FOR BEAUTY PROFESSIONALS

Familiarize yourself with Florida's licensing requirements for beauty professionals. Understand the process of obtaining and maintaining your license, which is essential for practicing your chosen beauty specialization.

**Florida Licensing Requirements for Beauty Professionals:**
The Florida Department of Business and Professional Regulation (DBPR) oversees the licensing requirements for beauty professionals in the state. To become a licensed beauty professional in Florida, individuals must meet specific educational and examination requirements. Here are the licensing requirements for different beauty specializations:

## Cosmetologists:

**Education:** Complete a minimum of 1,200 hours of cosmetology education from a state-approved beauty school.

**Examination:** Pass the Florida Board of Cosmetology examination, which includes both written and practical (hands-on) components.

**Reciprocity:** Florida has reciprocity agreements with some other states, allowing licensed cosmetologists from those states to apply for a Florida license without taking the state examination.

## Estheticians:

**Education:** Complete a minimum of 220 hours of esthetics education from a state-approved beauty school.

**Examination:** Not required the Florida Board of Cosmetology examination for estheticians, which includes both written and practical components.

**Reciprocity:** Florida may grant licensure to estheticians from other states that have equivalent or greater education and examination requirements.

## Nail Technicians:

**Education:** Complete a minimum of 180 hours of nail technology education from a state-approved beauty school.

**Examination:** Not required the Florida Board of Cosmetology examination for nail technicians, which includes both written and practical components.

**Reciprocity:** Nail technicians from other states may be eligible for licensure in Florida based on reciprocity agreements.

**Examination:** Not required the Florida Board of Cosmetology examination for full specialists, which includes both written and practical components.

**Barbers:**

**Education:** Complete a minimum of 600 to 900 hours of barber education from a state-approved barber school.

**Examination:** Pass the Florida Board of Barbering examination, which includes both written and practical components.

**Reciprocity:** Licensed barbers from other states may be eligible for licensure in Florida based on reciprocity agreements.

**Specialty Licenses (e.g., Hair Braiders, Body Wrappers):**

Requirements vary for specialty licenses. Some may require completing a certain number of hours of specialized education, passing an examination, or meeting other specific criteria.

After meeting the educational and examination requirements, applicants must submit an application to the Florida DBPR and pay the necessary fees. Once licensed, beauty professionals must adhere to continuing education requirements to renew their licenses periodically.

It's crucial for admission representatives to inform prospective students about these licensing requirements and emphasize the importance of attending a state-approved beauty school to ensure eligibility for licensure. Providing accurate information about the licensing process prepares students for a successful career in the beauty industry in Florida.

# PREPARING FOR STATE BOARD EXAMINATIONS

Prepare for the state board examinations, a crucial step in becoming a licensed beauty professional. We'll provide resources and strategies to ensure you're ready to excel in these examinations.

As an admission representative, your primary goal is to support and guide prospective beauty school students throughout their journey. Preparing students for State Board Examinations is a crucial aspect of your role, as it directly impacts their future careers in the beauty industry.

**Here's how you can use this knowledge in your career as an admission representative:**

**Empower Prospective Students:**

By understanding the State Board Examination requirements and preparation strategies, you can empower potential students with valuable information. This knowledge will help them make informed decisions about their beauty school education and the path towards becoming licensed professionals.

**Highlight the Importance of Licensing:**

Emphasize the significance of obtaining a professional license in the beauty industry. Explain to potential students that becoming licensed not only opens doors to various job opportunities but also ensures their competence and adherence to industry standards.

**Promote the School's Examination Preparation Resources:**

Utilize your knowledge to promote the examination preparation resources offered by the beauty school. Highlight the availability of study materials, mock exams, and guidance from experienced instructors to help students excel in their State Board Examinations.

**Address Student Concerns:**

Many prospective students may be apprehensive about the licensing process. By being well-versed in the examination requirements, you can address their concerns and provide reassurance. This will instill confidence in their decision to pursue a beauty school education.

**Customize Guidance:**

Use your knowledge of State Board Examination requirements to customize guidance for individual students. Tailor your advice based on their chosen specialization and any specific areas they may need extra support in.

**Create a Supportive Environment:**

Foster a supportive environment for potential students by offering encouragement and motivating them to excel in their studies. Knowing that you are well-informed about the examination process will boost their trust in your guidance.

**Advocate for Success:**

Demonstrate your commitment to students' success by proactively helping them prepare for State Board Examinations. This advocacy will build positive relationships with students and may even lead to referrals and positive word-of-mouth about the beauty school.

**Stay Updated with Changes:**

Keep yourself updated with any changes to State Board Examination requirements or processes. This ensures that the information you provide to students is accurate and current.

Using your knowledge of State Board Examinations as an admission representative will not only assist prospective students in their preparation but also showcase your expertise and dedication to their success. By guiding students through this critical aspect of their beauty school journey, you can make a significant impact on their future careers in the beauty industry and contribute to the overall success of the beauty school you represent.

# CONTINUING EDUCATION

Discover the importance of continuing education in the beauty industry. We'll guide you through opportunities to enhance your skills and knowledge throughout your career.

Continuing education is a vital aspect of the beauty industry, and as admissions representatives, it's essential to communicate its importance to prospective students. Continuing education offers beauty professionals opportunities to stay relevant, update their skills, and remain competitive in the ever-evolving beauty landscape.

Here's how you can highlight the significance of continuing education to potential students:

**Adapting to Industry Trends:**

Emphasize that the beauty industry is continuously evolving, with new trends, techniques, and technologies emerging regularly. Continuing education allows beauty professionals to stay up-to-date with the latest trends and adapt their skills to meet the changing demands of clients.

**Mastering New Techniques:**

Continuing education programs offer advanced training in specialized areas, such as advanced hairstyling techniques, innovative makeup application, cutting-edge skincare treatments, or eco-friendly beauty practices. These opportunities can help beauty professionals elevate their expertise and expand their service offerings.

**Enhancing Career Opportunities:**

Continuing education opens doors to higher-level positions and increased career opportunities. Professionals who invest in ongoing learning are often more sought after by employers and clients, leading to better job prospects and potentially higher earning potential.

**Building Confidence:**

By enrolling in continuing education courses, beauty professionals gain confidence in their abilities. This newfound confidence translates into better client interactions and an increased ability to handle diverse beauty challenges.

**Networking and Industry Connections:**

Continuing education programs often provide networking opportunities, allowing beauty professionals to connect with industry experts and like-minded peers. These connections can lead to valuable collaborations, mentorship, and exposure to new career possibilities.

**Meeting Licensing Requirements:**

Many states, including Florida, have continuing education requirements for maintaining professional licenses in the beauty industry. It's essential to inform potential students that participating in continuing education ensures they meet these regulatory obligations and can continue practicing legally.

**Specializations and Certifications:**

Continuing education often offers certifications in specialized areas, such as eyelash extensions, bridal makeup, or advanced skincare treatments. These certifications showcase a professional's dedication to their craft and can attract a broader clientele.

**Investing in Personal Growth:**

Continuing education goes beyond acquiring technical skills; it also fosters personal growth and a passion for lifelong learning. Encourage potential students to view continuing education as an investment in their personal and professional development.

**Staying Compliant with Health and Safety Standards:**

As the beauty industry prioritizes client safety and hygiene, continuing education provides updates on health and safety practices, ensuring professionals adhere to the latest regulations and protocols.

## Fulfilling Client Expectations:

Clients today expect beauty professionals to be knowledgeable and capable of delivering top-notch services. Continuing education empowers professionals to exceed client expectations and provide exceptional experiences.

By highlighting the benefits of continuing education, admissions representatives can inspire potential students to value ongoing learning as an essential part of their beauty career. Encourage them to see continuing education as an opportunity to excel, grow, and remain at the forefront of the beauty industry throughout their entire career journey.

# SETTLING INTO BEAUTY SCHOOL LIFE

## ADJUSTING TO CAMPUS LIFE

Navigate the transition into beauty school life smoothly. From getting to know your classmates to finding a balance between academics and social activities, we'll help you settle into your new environment.

As an admissions representative, it is crucial to support prospective students not only through the admissions process but also as they adjust to campus life. The transition into beauty school can be both exciting and challenging, and your guidance can help students settle into their new environment smoothly. Here's how you can help prospective students navigate this transition:

**Orientation and Welcome:**

Provide information about the school's orientation program and the resources available to help new students acclimate to campus life. Emphasize that the school is dedicated to providing a welcoming and supportive environment.

**Encourage Socialization:**

Encourage students to get to know their classmates and participate in social activities. Making friends and building a network of supportive peers can enhance their overall experience and create a sense of belonging.

**Time Management Skills:**

Emphasize the importance of time management in balancing academics and social activities. Share tips on how to prioritize tasks, create study schedules, and make time for socializing and self-care.

**Utilize Support Services:**

Inform students about the various support services available on campus, such as academic advising, counseling, and tutoring. Encourage them to seek help if they encounter challenges academically or personally.

**Explore Campus Facilities:**

Guide students on how to familiarize themselves with campus facilities, including classrooms, laboratories, libraries, and recreational areas. Knowing their way around campus can boost their confidence and comfort level.

**Involvement in Campus Clubs and Organizations:**

Promote campus clubs and organizations related to the beauty industry or other interests. Joining clubs can provide students with opportunities for networking, skill-building, and personal growth.

**Cultural Diversity and Inclusion:**

Emphasize the value of embracing cultural diversity and fostering an inclusive campus community.

Highlight events or initiatives that promote diversity and inclusivity.

## Managing Homesickness:

Acknowledge that some students may experience homesickness, especially if they are from out of town. Provide tips on coping with homesickness and reassure them that it is normal to feel this way during the adjustment period.

## Safety and Campus Security:

Educate students about campus safety and security measures. Knowing that their safety is a priority can help ease concerns and allow them to focus on their studies and social interactions.

## Self-Care and Wellness:

Stress the importance of self-care and maintaining a healthy work-life balance. Encourage students to engage in activities that promote their physical and mental well-being.

By addressing these aspects from the admissions representatives' perspective, you can help potential students feel more confident and prepared as they transition into beauty school life. Your support and guidance will play a significant role in their overall satisfaction with their beauty school experience, contributing to a positive and fulfilling journey throughout their time on campus.

# BALANCING ACADEMICS AND PRACTICAL TRAINING

Find the right balance between classroom learning and practical hands-on training. Learn how to optimize your learning experience and make the most of the opportunities provided by your beauty school.

As an admissions representative, it's essential to guide prospective students on how to strike the right balance between academics and practical hands-on training in beauty school. Achieving this balance is key to optimizing the learning experience and making the most of the opportunities provided by the beauty school. Here's how you can help students navigate this aspect:

**Understanding the Curriculum:**

Provide a detailed overview of the beauty school's curriculum, highlighting the blend of theoretical and practical components. Explain how each aspect contributes to their overall education and skill development.

**Recognizing the Value of Both:**

Emphasize that classroom learning provides the theoretical foundation necessary to understand concepts and techniques.

Highlight the importance of practical hands-on training, as it allows students to apply their knowledge, gain confidence, and refine their skills.

## Time Management:

Guide students on effective time management to ensure they allocate sufficient time to both academics and practical training. Encourage them to create study schedules and practice routines to maximize their learning experience.

## Participating Actively in Class:

Encourage students to actively engage in classroom discussions and activities. Active participation helps reinforce theoretical concepts and fosters a deeper understanding of the subject matter.

## Taking Advantage of Practical Opportunities:

Remind students to take full advantage of hands-on training opportunities. Encourage them to practice on models or mannequins provided by the school and seek additional practice outside of class if needed.

Promote engagement with real clients during salon days or supervised practice, as this allows students to gain valuable experience and build their portfolios.

## Asking for Feedback and Support:

Encourage students to seek feedback from instructors during both theoretical lessons and practical sessions. Constructive feedback helps students identify areas for improvement and make necessary adjustments.

## Creating a Supportive Learning Environment:

Advocate for a supportive learning environment where students feel comfortable asking questions and seeking guidance from instructors and peers. This atmosphere fosters a positive and nurturing learning experience.

**Maintaining a Growth Mindset:**

Instill a growth mindset in students, encouraging them to view challenges as opportunities for growth. Remind them that learning is a continuous process, and each experience, whether success or setback, contributes to their development.

**Balancing Practice and Study Groups:**

Suggest the formation of study groups or practice groups, where students can collaborate, practice together, and share knowledge. Peer learning can be beneficial in reinforcing concepts and gaining new insights.

**Staying Organized:**

Emphasize the importance of staying organized, keeping track of assignments, and planning ahead for practical sessions. Being organized reduces stress and ensures that students make the most of their learning opportunities.

By offering guidance on balancing academics and practical training, you empower students to optimize their learning experience in beauty school. The right balance between theory and practice sets the foundation for a successful and rewarding journey in the beauty industry, enabling students to graduate with the confidence and competence needed to excel in their chosen career paths.

# BUILDING A SUPPORTIVE BEAUTY SCHOOL COMMUNITY

Cultivate meaningful connections with your peers, instructors, and staff members. Discover the value of a supportive beauty school community and how it can positively impact your personal and professional growth.

As an admissions representative, one of your roles is to convey the value of building a supportive beauty school community to prospective students. Cultivating meaningful connections with peers, instructors, and staff members is essential for a positive and enriching beauty school experience. Here's how you can emphasize the importance of a supportive beauty school community:

**Creating a Welcoming Environment:**

Highlight that a supportive beauty school community starts with a welcoming and inclusive environment. Emphasize that the school is committed to fostering a sense of belonging for all students.

**Collaboration and Peer Learning:**

Showcase the benefits of collaboration and peer learning within the beauty school community. Encourage students to work together, share knowledge, and support one another in their learning journey.

**Access to Experienced Instructors:**

Stress the importance of connecting with experienced instructors and the value of their guidance and mentorship. Instructors play a crucial role in students' personal and professional growth.

**Networking Opportunities:**

Promote the networking opportunities available within the beauty school community. Explain that connecting with industry professionals and alumni can open doors to potential job opportunities and career advancement.

**Learning from Diverse Perspectives:**

Emphasize that a supportive beauty school community embraces diversity and allows students to learn from diverse perspectives and experiences. This exposure enriches their understanding of the beauty industry and prepares them for real-world interactions.

**Encouraging Personal Growth:**

Highlight that a supportive community encourages personal growth and self-discovery. Students are more likely to explore their passions and talents when they feel supported by their peers and instructors.

**Mental and Emotional Well-being:**

Advocate for a school culture that prioritizes mental and emotional well-being. Stress that a supportive community provides a safe space for students to seek help, share challenges, and receive encouragement.

**Teamwork and Camaraderie:**

Emphasize the importance of teamwork and camaraderie in the beauty industry. Explain that beauty professionals often work in team settings, and developing strong collaborative skills in school can benefit their future careers.

## Celebrating Success and Progress:

Communicate that a supportive beauty school community celebrates the success and progress of its members. Recognizing achievements, no matter how small, boosts motivation and confidence.

## Long-lasting Connections:

Stress the potential for long-lasting connections and friendships formed within the beauty school community. Remind students that these connections can extend beyond graduation, providing ongoing support and professional relationships.

By conveying the value of a supportive beauty school community, you inspire prospective students to seek an environment that nurtures personal and professional growth. A strong and supportive community can positively impact students' confidence, skill development, and overall satisfaction during their beauty school journey. As admissions representatives, your advocacy for a nurturing environment can contribute to creating a positive and inclusive culture that benefits everyone within the beauty school community.

# CAREER OPPORTUNITIES AND JOB PLACEMENT

## EXPLORING CAREER PATHWAYS IN THE BEAUTY INDUSTRY

Explore the diverse career pathways available in the beauty industry. From working in salons and spas to pursuing freelance opportunities or entrepreneurship, we'll guide you through the possibilities.

As an admissions representative, one of your key objectives is to help prospective students explore the diverse career pathways available in the beauty industry. By providing information about various career options, you can assist students in making informed decisions about their educational journey. Here's how you can guide them through the possibilities:

**Career Exploration:**

Emphasize the importance of exploring different career pathways within the beauty industry. Encourage students to consider their interests, strengths, and aspirations when evaluating potential career options.

**Salon and Spa Careers:**

Highlight the traditional career path of working in salons and spas. Explain the different roles available, such as hairstylists, estheticians, nail technicians, and makeup artists. Describe the day-to-day responsibilities and potential for growth in these settings.

**Specialized Fields:**

Introduce students to specialized fields within the beauty industry, such as bridal makeup, special effects makeup, medical esthetics, or high-fashion hairstyling. Discuss the opportunities and potential demand for professionals in these niches.

**Freelancing and Self-Employment:**

Discuss the possibility of pursuing a freelance career, where beauty professionals can work independently and offer their services to clients. Explain the benefits of flexibility and autonomy in freelancing.

**Entrepreneurship:**

Showcase the path of entrepreneurship for those interested in starting their own beauty-related businesses. Discuss the essential steps involved in launching and managing a successful beauty business.

## Platform Opportunities:

Introduce students to the world of digital platforms and social media, where beauty influencers and content creators can build a brand and reach a global audience. Highlight the importance of creativity and personal branding in this area.

## Educator and Trainer Roles:

Discuss the career opportunities in education and training within the beauty industry. Explain how experienced professionals can become educators or trainers in beauty schools, workshops, or corporate settings.

## Advanced Certifications and Continuing Education:

Emphasize the value of advanced certifications and continuing education in opening doors to higher-level positions and specialized career paths. Discuss how ongoing learning can enhance career opportunities.

## Industry Trends and Innovations:

Keep students updated on industry trends, innovations, and emerging career opportunities. Encourage them to stay informed about new techniques, products, and technologies that may shape their career choices.

## Guest Speakers and Alumni Success Stories:

Invite guest speakers from diverse career backgrounds and successful alumni to share their career journeys with prospective students. Real-life examples can inspire and provide valuable insights.

By guiding prospective students through the various career pathways in the beauty industry, you empower them to make informed choices about their education and future. As admissions representatives, your objective is to inspire and support students in pursuing their passions and achieving their career goals within the dynamic and rewarding world of beauty.

# JOB PLACEMENT SERVICES AND RESOURCES

Discover the job placement services and resources offered by beauty schools in Florida. Learn how these resources can support you in finding employment upon graduation.

Job placement services and resources are essential components of a comprehensive beauty school education. These services are designed to assist students in finding employment opportunities upon graduation and launching their careers in the beauty industry. As an admissions representative, it's crucial to inform prospective students about the job placement services and resources offered by beauty schools in Florida. Here's how you can explain their significance:

**Career Guidance and Counseling:**

> Highlight that beauty schools provide career guidance and counseling services to help students identify their career goals and aspirations. Career counselors can assist students in aligning their skills and interests with specific job opportunities.

## Resume Writing and Interview Preparation:

Inform students that beauty schools often offer assistance with resume writing and interview preparation. This support helps students present themselves professionally to potential employers and enhances their chances of securing job offers.

## Industry Partnerships and Job Connections:

Emphasize that beauty schools in Florida typically have strong connections with local salons, spas, and beauty establishments. These partnerships can lead to job placement opportunities and potential internships during or after their education.

## Job Fairs and Networking Events:

Discuss the job fairs and networking events organized by beauty schools, where students can meet industry professionals and potential employers. These events create networking opportunities and expose students to a wide range of job prospects.

## Alumni Networks:

Mention the value of alumni networks within the beauty school community. Graduates often maintain connections with their alma mater and may offer job opportunities or mentorship to recent graduates.

## Online Job Boards and Listings:

Explain that beauty schools may have access to exclusive online job boards and listings that cater specifically to the beauty industry. These platforms can connect students with job openings in salons, spas, resorts, and other beauty-related businesses.

## Mock Interviews and Feedback:

Inform students that beauty schools might conduct mock interviews to help them practice and refine their interview skills. Constructive feedback from instructors and career counselors can improve their interview performance.

## Job Placement Assistance Beyond Graduation:

Reassure students that job placement assistance is not limited to immediate post-graduation. Beauty schools may continue to provide support and resources as graduates advance in their careers or seek new opportunities.

## Industry Updates and Job Market Trends:

Discuss how beauty schools keep students informed about industry updates and job market trends. Staying informed about the ever-changing beauty industry can help students adapt and find opportunities in high-demand areas.

## Tailored Job Search Strategies:

Highlight that career counselors work with individual students to develop tailored job search strategies based on their interests, skills, and preferred work settings.

By explaining the job placement services and resources available, you empower prospective students to see beauty schools as more than just places of education. They become valuable partners in their journey toward a successful and fulfilling career in the beauty industry. Students can gain confidence knowing that support is available to help them transition from the classroom to the workforce with the skills and knowledge needed to thrive in their chosen profession.

# CHALLENGES AND OPPORTUNITIES IN THE BEAUTY INDUSTRY

## ADDRESSING COMMON CHALLENGES IN BEAUTY SCHOOL

Recognize common challenges faced by beauty school students and how to overcome them. From time management issues to maintaining motivation, we'll offer strategies for success.

As an admissions representative, part of your role is to address common challenges faced by beauty school students and provide strategies to help them overcome these obstacles. By acknowledging these challenges and offering guidance, you can support students in their journey towards success. Here's how you can assist students in addressing common challenges in beauty school:

**Time Management:**

Recognize that beauty school can be demanding, and students may struggle to balance their academic commitments with practical training and personal life. Offer time management tips, such as creating schedules, setting priorities, and breaking tasks into manageable chunks.

**Motivation and Burnout:**

Acknowledge that students may experience periods of low motivation or burnout, especially when facing rigorous training and coursework. Encourage students to set realistic goals, celebrate small successes, and take breaks to avoid burnout.

**Academic Support:**

Inform students about the academic support services available, such as tutoring, study groups, or one-on-one help from instructors. Let them know that seeking assistance is a sign of dedication to their education and growth.

**Financial Concerns:**

Recognize that financial stress can be a common challenge for students. Offer information about financial aid options, scholarships, and part-time job opportunities to ease the burden of educational expenses.

**Personal Confidence:**

Address potential issues with self-confidence that students may face, particularly when performing beauty services on real clients. Encourage practice, provide positive feedback, and remind students that building confidence is a gradual process.

**Handling Constructive Criticism:**

Acknowledge that receiving constructive criticism from instructors or peers can be challenging. Teach students how to view feedback as an opportunity for improvement and growth rather than a personal setback.

**Cultural and Language Barriers:**

Be sensitive to the needs of students from diverse backgrounds, including those with language barriers. Promote an inclusive environment and offer additional support, such as language assistance or cultural resources.

**Stress Management:**

Provide stress management techniques to help students cope with the pressures of beauty school. Techniques may include mindfulness exercises, relaxation techniques, and engaging in hobbies or physical activities.

**Navigating Industry Competition:**

Acknowledge that the beauty industry can be competitive. Encourage students to focus on their unique strengths, continuous learning, and building a strong professional network to stand out in the field.

**Building a Supportive Network:**

> Emphasize the importance of building a supportive network of classmates, instructors, and industry professionals. A sense of community can help students feel connected and motivated throughout their beauty school journey.

By addressing these common challenges and providing strategies for success, you can help students overcome obstacles and stay focused on their beauty school goals. Your guidance and support as an admissions representative will play a vital role in ensuring that students have a positive and fulfilling experience in beauty school, leading them toward a successful career in the beauty industry.

# EMBRACING DIVERSITY AND INCLUSIVITY

Explore the importance of diversity and inclusivity in the beauty industry. Learn how embracing differences can enrich your learning experience and enhance your professional approach.

As an admissions representative, it's crucial to emphasize the importance of diversity and inclusivity in the beauty industry to prospective students. Embracing differences, whether in terms of ethnicity, culture, gender, or background, is not only a fundamental value but also a source of enrichment for both the learning experience and the professional approach of future beauty professionals. Here's how you can promote the significance of diversity and inclusivity:

**Reflecting the Real World:**

Explain that the beauty industry serves a diverse clientele with varying skin tones, hair types, and beauty needs. Embracing diversity in beauty education prepares students to cater to the real-world needs of clients from all walks of life.

**Learning from Different Perspectives:**

Emphasize that a diverse learning environment exposes students to different perspectives and approaches to beauty. Students can learn from their peers' unique experiences and cultural practices, broadening their knowledge and creativity.

**Cultural Sensitivity and Awareness:**

Highlight the importance of cultural sensitivity and awareness in the beauty industry. Discuss how understanding and respecting cultural practices can foster positive client relationships and prevent misunderstandings.

**Creating Inclusive Spaces:**

Promote the creation of inclusive spaces within the beauty school, where students feel accepted and celebrated for their individuality. Encourage students to support and uplift one another, fostering a positive and supportive community.

**Breaking Stereotypes:**

Address beauty industry stereotypes and biases that may exist. Encourage students to challenge these preconceptions and redefine beauty standards to be inclusive and representative of diverse beauty ideals.

### Adapting Techniques for All:

Discuss how embracing diversity involves learning to adapt beauty techniques to suit clients of different backgrounds and needs. This adaptability is a valuable skill in building a successful and diverse clientele.

### Building Empathy and Compassion:

Explain how exposure to diverse perspectives can foster empathy and compassion in beauty professionals. Understanding different experiences helps students approach their clients with understanding and care.

### Building a Diverse Clientele:

Share the benefits of a diverse clientele, including opportunities to expand one's skills, gain word-of-mouth referrals, and develop a strong reputation for being inclusive and accommodating.

### Addressing Cultural Appropriation:

Educate students on the importance of avoiding cultural appropriation in the beauty industry. Teach them to appreciate and respect cultural practices without appropriating or misrepresenting them.

### Promoting Social Change:

Remind students that embracing diversity and inclusivity in their professional approach can contribute to positive social change within the beauty industry and society as a whole.

By fostering a culture of diversity and inclusivity in beauty school, admissions representatives can attract students who value these principles and wish to contribute to a more inclusive and representative beauty industry. Emphasizing the importance of diversity not only enriches the learning experience but also prepares students to become compassionate and adaptable beauty professionals, ready to serve diverse communities with professionalism and respect.

# TRENDS AND INNOVATIONS SHAPING THE FUTURE OF BEAUTY

Stay informed about the latest trends and innovations shaping the beauty industry's future. Discover how staying current with technological advancements can set you apart as a forward-thinking beauty professional.

As an admissions representative, it is essential to keep prospective students informed about the latest trends and innovations shaping the future of the beauty industry. Staying current with technological advancements and industry trends is not only beneficial for students' education but also crucial for their success as beauty professionals. Here's how you can explore this topic with potential students:

**Introduction to Beauty Industry Trends:**

Begin by introducing students to the dynamic nature of the beauty industry. Explain that beauty trends are constantly evolving, influenced by changing consumer preferences, cultural shifts, and technological advancements.

## Role of Technology in Beauty:

Discuss the significant impact of technology on the beauty industry. Mention innovations such as virtual reality (VR) makeup applications, artificial intelligence (AI)-driven skincare analysis, and social media marketing techniques that are reshaping the way beauty services are delivered and marketed.

## Digital Marketing and Branding:

Emphasize the importance of digital marketing and online branding for beauty professionals. Teach students about creating engaging content, leveraging social media platforms, and building a strong online presence to reach a broader audience.

## Sustainable Beauty Practices:

Address the growing trend of sustainability in the beauty industry. Inform students about eco-friendly and cruelty-free beauty practices, as well as the increasing demand for sustainable products and packaging.

## Inclusive Beauty and Representation:

Discuss the shift towards more inclusive beauty standards and representation in the industry. Teach students about the importance of offering a diverse range of beauty products and services that cater to individuals of all skin tones, genders, and cultural backgrounds.

## Advancements in Skincare and Ingredients:

Inform students about the latest breakthroughs in skincare technology and ingredients. Topics may include the use of advanced serums, natural botanicals, and clean beauty formulations.

## Haircare Innovations:

Explore the advancements in haircare, such as innovative hair treatments, scalp analysis tools, and products tailored to different hair types and concerns.

## Specializations and Niche Services:

Introduce students to emerging specializations within the beauty industry, such as microblading, lash extensions, men's grooming, and medical aesthetics. Explain how pursuing niche services can lead to unique career opportunities.

## Adapting to Change:

Emphasize the importance of adaptability and continuous learning in the beauty industry. Encourage students to stay open-minded and willing to embrace new techniques and practices throughout their careers.

## Industry Insights and Guest Speakers:

Invite industry professionals and guest speakers who are experts in specific beauty trends and innovations. Their insights can provide students with valuable real-world perspectives and inspire them to stay curious and up-to-date.

By exploring the trends and innovations shaping the future of the beauty industry, admissions representatives can attract students who are excited about being part of a dynamic and forward-thinking field. Demonstrating a commitment to keeping students informed about the latest industry developments ensures they are well-prepared to thrive in a competitive and ever-evolving beauty landscape.

# CONCLUSION
## YOUR JOURNEY TO BEAUTY SCHOOL SUCCESS

Congratulations on completing this comprehensive guide to beauty school admissions in Florida! As you embark on your journey into the beauty industry, remember that your passion, dedication, and creativity will be the keys to your success.

As an admissions representative, it is essential to convey a sense of celebration and encouragement to prospective students who have completed the comprehensive guide to beauty school admissions in Florida. This message serves to inspire and motivate students as they embark on their journey into the beauty industry. Here's how you can explore this topic from the admissions representatives' perspectives:

**Celebrating Their Achievement:**

Start by congratulating students on completing the guide and taking the first step towards their dream of entering the beauty industry. Acknowledge their commitment to learning and pursuing a career in the beauty field.

**Emphasizing the Power of Passion:**

Remind students that passion for their chosen field is a driving force for success. Encourage them to tap into their passion for beauty and use it as a source of inspiration throughout their journey.

**Stressing the Value of Dedication:**
Emphasize that dedication and hard work are key components of achieving success in the beauty industry. Encourage students to stay focused on their goals and be persistent in their pursuit of excellence.

**Unlocking Creativity:**
Highlight the importance of creativity in the beauty industry. Explain that creativity is not only about artistic skills but also about innovative thinking and problem-solving. Encourage students to nurture their creativity and use it to offer unique and outstanding services.

**Being Open to Learning:**
Encourage students to maintain an open mindset and be receptive to learning new techniques, industry trends, and business strategies. Lifelong learning is crucial for personal and professional growth.

**Building a Supportive Network:**
Remind students to surround themselves with a supportive network of peers, instructors, and industry professionals. A strong support system can provide valuable guidance and encouragement throughout their beauty school journey.

**Persevering Through Challenges:**
Acknowledge that challenges may arise along the way, but reassure students that they have the resilience and determination to overcome them. Encourage them to view challenges as opportunities for growth and learning.

**Embracing Diversity and Inclusivity:**

Reinforce the importance of embracing diversity and inclusivity in the beauty industry. Encourage students to celebrate and respect the uniqueness of each client they serve.

**Staying Updated on Industry Trends:**

Stress the significance of staying informed about industry trends and innovations. Encourage students to seek out educational resources, attend workshops, and connect with industry professionals to stay current in their field.

**Setting Goals and Visualizing Success:**

Encourage students to set clear goals for their beauty school journey and beyond. Visualization can be a powerful tool in manifesting success and achieving their aspirations.

By sharing this message, admissions representatives can instill a sense of confidence and excitement in prospective students as they begin their beauty school journey. Supporting students with positive affirmations and emphasizing the importance of passion, dedication, and creativity sets the stage for a fulfilling and successful career in the beauty industry.

# GLOSSARY OF BEAUTY SCHOOL TERMS

Refer to a handy glossary that defines key terms and concepts relevant to the beauty industry and beauty school education.

**Accreditation:** *The process of certification and recognition by a professional body or agency that evaluates and ensures the quality and standards of education provided by a beauty school.*

**Aesthetics:** *The study and practice of beauty, focusing on skincare, facials, and other treatments that promote healthy and glowing skin.*

**Apprenticeship:** *A hands-on training program where a student works under the guidance of an experienced beauty professional to gain practical skills.*

**Barbering:** *A specialized area of beauty that focuses on men's grooming, including haircuts, beard trims, and facial hair styling.*

**Cosmetology:** *A comprehensive beauty program that includes haircare, skincare, nail care, and makeup application.*

**Esthetics:** *Also known as skincare, esthetics focuses on skin treatments, facials, and other services to improve and maintain skin health.*

**Licensing Requirements:** *The specific criteria and qualifications individuals must meet to become licensed beauty professionals, which may vary by state.*

**Manicure:** *The grooming and beautification of nails, including trimming, shaping, and applying nail polish.*

**Microblading:** *A semi-permanent eyebrow enhancement technique involving precise, hair-like strokes to mimic natural eyebrows.*

**Nail Technician:** *A beauty professional specializing in nail care, including manicures, pedicures, and nail extensions.*

**Pedicure:** *The grooming and beautification of feet and toenails, including exfoliation, massage, and nail polish application.*

**Salon:** *An establishment where beauty services such as haircuts, styling, and skincare treatments are offered.*

**Spa:** *A facility that provides relaxation and beauty services, such as massages, facials, and body treatments.*

**Specialization:** *Focusing on a specific area within the beauty industry, such as makeup artistry, hair colorist, or spa management.*

**Stylist:** *A generic term for a beauty professional who performs hair services, such as cutting, styling, and coloring.*

**Tuition:** *The cost of attending beauty school, including fees for classes, materials, and supplies.*

**Waxing:** *A hair removal technique using heated wax to remove unwanted hair from various parts of the body.*

**Workshop:** *A short, intensive training session where students can learn specific techniques or skills from experienced professionals.*

**Portfolio:** *A collection of a beauty professional's best work, often used to showcase their skills and creativity to potential clients or employers.*

**Continuing Education:** *Ongoing learning and professional development to stay updated on industry trends and advance skills and knowledge.*

This glossary provides a basic understanding of key terms and concepts in the beauty industry and beauty school education. Students can use this as a quick reference to familiarize themselves with essential terminology throughout their beauty school journey.

# RECOMMENDED READING AND WEBSITES

Access a curated list of recommended reading materials and websites to further expand your knowledge of the beauty industry and enhance your academic journey.

As an admissions representative seeking to expand your knowledge of the beauty industry and enhance your skills, here is a curated list of recommended reading materials and websites:

## READING MATERIALS:

*"Milady Standard Cosmetology" by Milady:* This comprehensive textbook covers all aspects of cosmetology, including haircare, skincare, nail care, and salon management.

*"Bobbi Brown Makeup Manual: For Everyone from Beginner to Pro" by Bobbi Brown:* A valuable resource for makeup artists and beauty professionals, offering tips, techniques, and insights from renowned makeup artist Bobbi Brown.

*"The Beauty Industry Survival Guide: A Salon Professional's Handbook" by Tina Alberino:* This book provides practical advice and business strategies for salon professionals, including marketing, client retention, and industry trends.

*"Esthetician's Guide to Client Safety and Wellness" by Tina Zillmann:* An essential read for estheticians, covering client safety, ethical practices, and maintaining a healthy work environment.

*"The Business of Beauty: Cosmetics Retailing in Modern America" by E. Rivlin:* This book explores the history and business aspects of the beauty industry in America, offering valuable insights into its evolution.

# WEBSITES:

*Professional Beauty Association (PBA) - Salon & Spa Professionals Resource:* A leading industry association that provides resources, education, and networking opportunities for salon and spa professionals.

*Beauty Industry Report:* This website offers news, trends, and insights into the beauty industry, including information on product launches, mergers, and industry innovations.

*American Association of Cosmetology Schools (AACS):* AACS provides information and resources for beauty school professionals, including best practices, policy updates, and industry research.

*Beauty Independent:* A digital publication focusing on independent beauty brands and industry innovation, providing valuable insights into the evolving beauty landscape.

***Beauty Launchpad:*** *A platform offering educational articles, tutorials, and trend reports for beauty professionals, including hair, makeup, and skincare.*

***Beauty Changes Lives:*** *A nonprofit organization that supports beauty industry education and scholarships, offering valuable resources for students and professionals.*

***Beauty Schools Directory:*** *A website that provides a directory of beauty schools across the country, helping prospective students find and compare educational programs.*

These reading materials and websites cover a wide range of topics, from technical knowledge to business insights and industry trends. Continuously exploring these resources will help you stay informed about the latest developments in the beauty industry and enhance your skills as an admissions representative. By being well-informed, you can better assist prospective students and provide valuable guidance for their beauty school journey.

GQ
PRESS

www.ingramcontent.com/pod-product-compliance
Lightning Source LLC
Chambersburg PA
CBHW031409250726
48656CB00002B/597